Camping Is Fun!

By Mikael Wesley

Illustrated by Nan Brooks

Target Skill *Review*
High-Frequency Words *Review*

Mom and Dad get set.

Max and Jen get set.

They get set to go on a trip.

The red tent will go in the van.

The pots will go in the van.

Max and Jen are in the red van.

They will set up camp.

Dad sets up the tent.

Max and Jen help Dad.

They go up a big hill.

Jen and Max see a nest.

Jen can see three eggs.

Look at the pond, Max.

Max can see a big bump.

What is it, Dad?

Mom sees a green frog.

Look at it jump.

It can jump a lot.

Jen and Max have fun.

It is fun to camp!